Learning Resource Centre

Barcode: 75080

To renew your loans:

Call: 01227 81 11 66
Email: lrc@eastkentcollege.ac.uk
Online: tiny.cc/renew-my-books

Please see below for the date your book is due back

1 4 NOV 2022

2/02/23

TAI CHI

FOR BODY, MIND & SPIRIT

A step-by-step guide to
achieving physical and
mental balance

Eric Chaline

WARD LOCK

First published in the UK 1998
by Ward Lock
Wellington House
125 Strand
London WC2R 0BB
A Cassell imprint

The credits that appear on page 128 are
hereby made a part of this copyright page.

A British Library Cataloguing in Publication Data block for
this book may be obtained from the British library.

ISBN 0 7063 7777 X

This book was designed and produced by
Quarto Publishing plc
The Old Brewery
6 Blundell Street
London N7 9BH

PROJECT EDITOR Ulla Weinberg
ART EDITOR Sally Bond
DESIGNER Vicki James
PHOTOGRAPHERS Paul Forrester, Lesley Howling
MODELS Victoria Kent, Brian Seabright, Ghislaine Picchio
PICTURE RESEARCHERS Gill
Metcalfe, Christine Lalla
ART DIRECTOR Moira Clinch
ASSISTANT ART DIRECTOR
Penny Cobb

Manufactured by Bright Arts
Pte Ltd, Singapore
Printed by Leefung-Asco
Printers Ltd, China

CONTENTS

INTRODUCTION

B Y PICKING THIS book off the shelf and reading these opening words, you have embarked on a journey. It may last a few months, a few years, or a whole lifetime; or it may end right now, as you decide that a practical philosophy of health and fitness, elaborated in China for the past two and a half thousand years, has nothing to offer you, and you snap the book shut.

Those of you who are still reading have several choices in the way you can approach tai chi: as a fighting technique, a healing art, a health and fitness exercise, a relaxation technique or as a spiritual meditation. *Tai Chi for Body, Mind & Spirit* touches on all of these aspects of tai chi, but it concentrates on the practical applications that maintain and improve your physical health and mental well-being.

Tai chi sword: There are many portals through which you can approach tai chi. In the past, one of the most common was through the study of the martial arts.

We are better fed, housed and cared for than any other humans in history, yet our very success has made us among the least fit and most stressed. Tai chi's unique combination of exercise for the mind, body and spirit is the ideal antidote to the stresses and strains of modern life.

WHY TAI CHI?

The many techniques of tai chi combine into a balanced system of exercise that addresses all areas of physical fitness: muscular strength, endurance, flexibility and breathing; as well as relaxation and mental fitness. Unlike any conventional health and fitness training method or sport, tai chi can be recommended to anyone, regardless of sex, age, health or level of fitness. And while it remains within reach of the unfit, it is challenging enough to tax the super-fit athlete or martial artist.

Although tai chi offers a completely practical program of physical training that is designed to raise your level of physical fitness, it is based on a view of human life, and its relationship to the Universe, that is profoundly different from our own. And just as it would be impossible to play football without knowing the rules of the game, it is impossible to get the full benefit of tai chi without understanding its philosophical bases: the concept of qi (also chi) or internal energy, and the theory of yin and yang.

SUBTLE LIFE FORCE

No one can tell you what makes your body live. Scientists have an explanation for how your brain thinks, how your lungs breathe air, and how your heart pumps blood around your body to nourish its cells, but they cannot say why life began in your body and what makes it continue. For two and a half thousand years, the Chinese have called this subtle life force qi (or chi).

The Chinese believe that we are born with a store of qi inherited from our parents, and that we acquire more on a daily basis from the food we eat and the air we breathe. Qi flows through the human body along lines known as "meridians," one corresponding to each of the major organs of the body. If there is an imbalance in the qi or a blockage in its flow along the meridians, we fall physically or mentally ill.

If you have trouble accepting the traditional Chinese view of qi, you could think of it as a prescientific explanation for the interconnectedness of the thousands of organic systems and complex physiological processes – the oxygenation of blood in our lungs, the electrical impulses in our brains and nervous system, the chemical transformations in our cells – that together give life to your body.

"The further one goes, the less one knows."

– TAO TEH CHING

Tai chi is infused with the spirit of the Tao – the Way. Life is a never-ending journey – a process in which we must always seek to balance the opposite forces of yin and yang to find fulfillment and happiness.

Traditional Chinese medical practitioners re-establish the balance of the qi in the yin and yang organs by manipulating the qi through acupuncture, herbal medicine, moxibustion and qigong.

BASIC PRINCIPLES

The second basic principle embodied in tai chi is the theory of yin and yang. Everything in the Universe, the theory explains, is made of pairs of opposites: light and dark, positive and negative, strength and weakness, male and female, which are in a constant state of movement and transformation. Yin and yang are represented by the circular diagram shown on the facing page, where the light half of the circle, yang, contains the seed of the dark half, yin, and vice versa. As soon as one side becomes too powerful, it initiates a transformation that will bring the opposite side into prominence.

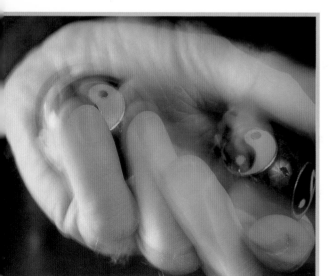

Yin and yan are in a constant state of flux and transformation, as symbolized by the yin-yang diagram.

In Chinese medical theory, the human body contains both yin and yang organs, and the mind and body are healthy as long as these are balanced by the qi. When a patient becomes ill, the Chinese doctor will not look for an external cause, such as a bacterial or viral agent, but for the reasons why the patient's qi, which is supposed to protect him from disease, has become weakened or unbalanced. Once he has identified the problem, he will prescribe a combination of therapies, including tai chi exercises known as the qigong (see pages 22–49), that will heal the patient, but not by treating his symptoms or attacking the external agent, but by encouraging the patient's ability to fight off the disease and cure himself. It is on this ability of the body to heal and strengthen itself that the techniques of tai chi are based.

OF MIND AND MATTER

Doctors have known for centuries that physical exercise can relieve the effects of mental depression. But how the mind affects the body is far from understood. Until prompted by the alternative therapies, Western medicine overlooked the fact that the mind–body link is a two-way street: When we are stressed and depressed, we often suffer from physical symptoms, such as tiredness, eating disorders, insomnia and weakened immunity to disease.

In contrast, traditional Chinese medicine is based on the view that the body and mind function as a holistic unit, and constantly influence one another. This relationship can be negative and result in ill-health, or positive and result in well-being. The great masters of tai chi concentrated on the latter. If there is a force – which they called qi – that regulates the functions of the body, they reasoned, it may be possible to cultivate

The universe is a constantly evolving process: night makes way for day, the seasons change, the generations succeed one another. To be truly happy we have to find our own balance in this sea of eternal change.

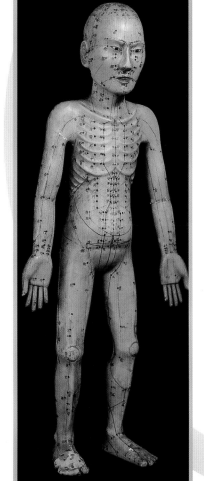

and increase it. What they and their followers discovered over the centuries is that the mind governs both the positive and negative aspects of qi. In the techniques they developed, which we now call tai chi, as you train your muscles and joints, you also use your most powerful organ – your mind, in the form of your imagination – to send a constant stream of positive, health-enhancing messages to your body. With every movement you make and every breath you take, you increase your store of health and well-being – qi – and circulate it around your body, increasing its strength and immunity to disease and aging.

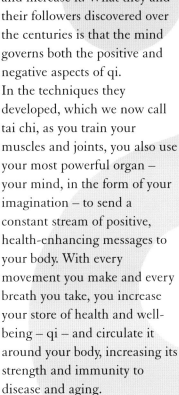
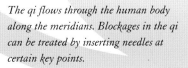

The qi flows through the human body along the meridians. Blockages in the qi can be treated by inserting needles at certain key points.

ORIGINS AND HISTORY

While the components of tai chi included in this book, the qigong exercises and the tai chi chuan form, share the same philosophical basis, they have widely differing origins. Qigong, the art of cultivating internal energy, has a history of over two and a half thousand years in China. It incorporates many hundreds of techniques, which can be divided into three categories: medical – to maintain health and cure disease; martial – to improve martial valor and fighting technique; and religious – to achieve spiritual enlightenment.

After the upheaval of the Cultural Revolution in China, when all traditional arts were banned, interest revived in traditional Chinese medicine and qigong therapies. This culminated in the 1980s with the formulation of a standardized sequence of tai chi qigong exercises to promote general physical health and mental well-being.

Tai chi chuan, which literally translated means "supreme ultimate fist," was first developed as a fighting art. Legend has it that it was created by Zhang Sanfeng, a 13th-century Taoist monk, while he was studying at the Shaolin Temple. The first historical reference to tai chi chuan as a separate martial art dates to the 17th century, when Chen Wangting created the Chen style. A student of the Chen style, Yang Luchan (1795–1872), the ablest martial artist of his day, founded the Yang style, which, as the basis for the simplified form, remains the most popular style of tai chi chuan today. The Chen and Yang styles gave rise to the Wu, Hao and Sun styles of tai chi chuan.

Banned for a period in communist China, tai chi chuan experienced a renaissance in the mid-1950s, when the simplified 24-step form was created and fast became one of the most widely practiced sports in mainland China.

> "*The mind and qi are king and the bones and muscles are the court.*"
>
> - SONG OF HAND PUSHING

"Silently treasure up knowledge and turn it over in the mind. Gradually you can do as you like."

- WANG ZONGYUE

PRACTICAL CONSIDERATIONS

The benefits of tai chi, like those of any other form of exercise, are cumulative. To help maintain your motivation, it is best to to decide on a fixed time of day for your practice, which can be at any time during the day; although you may find that morning practice of the qigong and form will energize you for the rest of the day, while performing the breathing and meditation exercises in the evening will help you unwind from the day's stresses. If practicing indoors, choose a quiet, well ventilated room with at least 40 sq.ft. (4 m²) of free space, and whenever your schedule and the weather permits, practice outdoors, in the park or your back yard. The only limitations for how much tai chi you should do are those set by the time available to you, but you should aim to practice for a minimum of 20 to 30 minutes daily.

You should wear loose clothes that do not constrict your waist or chest, making breathing difficult, nor impede the free movement of your limbs. Make sure that the clothes you pick are appropriate for the season. It is advisable to wear footwear, especially if practicing outdoors. Choose comfortable flat-soled slippers or shoes that are firmly attached to your foot and give you a stable footing, while allowing you to feel the ground.

Spiraling Arms - Body in Motion

FROM THE macrocosm of the planet's orbit around the sun to the microcosm of the electron's path around the nucleus of the atom, nature moves in spirals. So, in tai chi, which seeks to follow the laws of natural motion, you will find neither straight lines nor right angles. When you perform the tai chi form and qigong exercises, your posture and movements should immediately suggest roundness: your chest is sunken, not puffed out; your arms and legs are relaxed and bent, never straight and stiff; your movements have the fluidity and smoothness of water, never hard or jerking.

Spiraling arms is a preparatory exercise that allows you to discover and explore the basic principles of tai chi motion and, as your skill increases, to monitor your progress. Do not

"In motion
all parts of the body must be
light, nimble
and strung together."

— ZHANG SANFENG

worry, if in the beginning, your movements lack coordination or do not exactly match the illustrations. It is more important that you find your body's center of gravity, and, keeping your mind fixed there, work to develop a smooth, continuous motion with which you feel completely comfortable. With practice, spiraling hands will become automatic; so, to ensure that your mind does not wander, always keep it focused on the movement.

"Tai chi chuan
is like a great river
rolling on unceasingly."

— ZHANG SANFENG

SPIRALING ARMS

Take two or three deep breaths to clear your mind and release the tensions in your body. Stand with your feet shoulder-width apart, with your front foot at right angles to your rear foot. With your back and head erect and your arms hanging loosely at your side, relax your knees and shift your weight slowly from your front to your rear foot.

1 Gently rocking backward and forward, raise your arms, keeping your shoulders, elbows and wrists relaxed, and make linked horizontal circles with your hands, palms facing down.

2 Without interrupting the flow of the movement, turn your waist in time to the spiraling of your arms and the shifting of your weight. Maintain a constant speed throughout the exercise, and keep your body at the same height, neither rising nor falling as you move.

3 Feel the connection between your feet, waist and shoulders in one seamless movement. In order to maintain the correct speed, imagine that you are performing the exercise underwater, which simultaneously supports you and slows you down.

4 Identify any stiffness or weakness in your body: Are your shoulders, neck or back becoming tense? Are your leg muscles aching and tired? These are areas that will require special attention during your further study of tai chi.

Opening the Energy Gates

In the morning of your practice, your muscles and joints are stiff and your bones are hollow. At noontime, the qi flows freely into your dantian; and in the evening of your practice the qi congeals in your marrow, turning it to steel.

Opening the Energy Gates

As you begin your practice of tai chi, you will notice that it shares many features familiar to you from other forms of exercise: wearing specialist clothing and shoes, going to a room or area set aside for practice, and performing preparatory warm-up exercises. In aerobics and weight-training, the main purpose of warming up and stretching is to protect you from injury, and any considerations of enhancing performance and enjoyment are secondary.

In tai chi, whose aim is to bring the mental and physical aspects of movement into complete harmony, a period of preparation to relax and prepare the mind and body is doubly necessary, and as your practice progresses, you may wish to perform meditation and breathing exercises before you begin your daily round of exercises.

The following movements are designed to stretch and mobilize your joints and major muscle groups, and they can be used with any other form of exercise you take part in, such as golf or tennis; however, for your tai chi practice, they also serve to clear any blockages in your qi and stimulate its flow throughout your body.

➤ **Rotating the elbows** Stand with your feet shoulder-width apart. Keeping your shoulders and upper back relaxed, make circles with your forearms, rotating from your elbows.

▲ Rotating the wrists
Keeping your shoulders and elbows relaxed, clasp your hands together in front of you and make a figure of eight in one direction. Repeat the movement in the opposite direction. Don't let tension build up in the muscles of your neck and upper back.

➤ As you rotate your forearms, rise onto the balls of your feet. Slowly raise and lower your body in time with the movement of your arms.

▼ **Rotating the shoulders** With your hands resting loosely on your shoulders, make circles with your elbows forward and then backward.

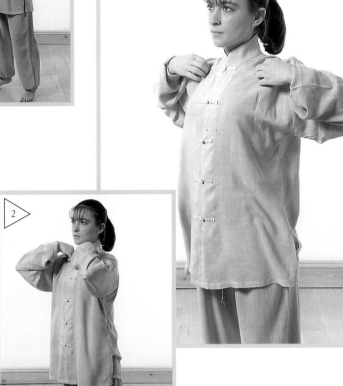

"Remember when moving there is no place that does not move."

- WU YUXIANG

▼ **Pulling back the arms** Slowly raise one arm while lowering the other. Repeat the movement twice.

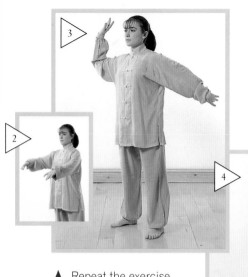

➤ **Rotating the hips** Stand with your legs shoulder-width apart. Put your hands on your hips, and rotate your body clockwise and counterclockwise for two full turns.

▲ Repeat the exercise with the movement of your arms reversed.

▼ **Rotating the ankles** Stand with your feet together, knees bent. Hold your knees as you rotate them one way and then the other.

▼ **Wild goose reaches for the sky** Stand with your feet shoulder-width apart, arms hanging loosely at your side. Breathe in, raise and open your arms toward the sky and rise to the balls of your feet. Hold the position momentarily, then breathe out as you lower your arms and body.

▲ Turning waist to swing arms
Turn your waist from left to right, shifting your weight from one foot to the other, as your arms swing freely.

➤ Turning step to swing arms
As you swing, raise one foot onto its heel and turn it out as the opposing arm swings forward. Your foot should be in position before your waist begins to turn.

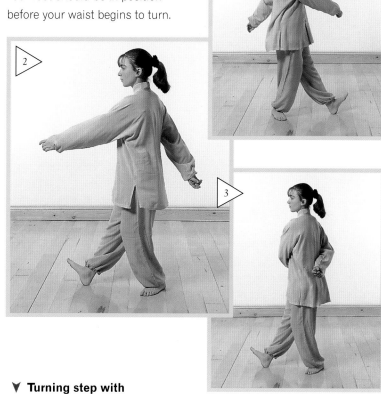

▲ Turning waist to pat the back
Still using the turning step, swing your hands over your shoulders and pat yourself lightly. Do not force a stretch in this movement, but go only as far as the swing naturally takes your hand.

▼ Turning step with walking swing Using the same turning step technique for your feet as in the previous exercises, swing the arms up to shoulder height and down in opposite directions, making two smooth, sweeping arcs.

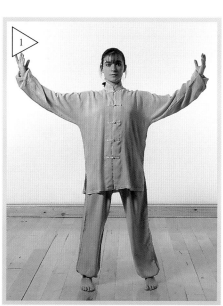

▼ Hamstring stretch Stand with your legs apart and take a step forward with your right foot, resting it on its heel. With your hands on your knees, bend forward from the waist. Repeat with the left foot.

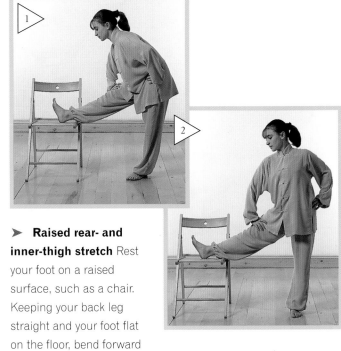

➤ Raised rear- and inner-thigh stretch Rest your foot on a raised surface, such as a chair. Keeping your back leg straight and your foot flat on the floor, bend forward to stretch your hamstring, then straighten your body, turn the waist to the front and bend sideways to stretch your inner thigh. Repeat the sequence with your other leg. Breathe out as you stretch forward and breathe in as you release the stretch.

➤ Rotating your ankles Resting your weight on your left foot, rotate your right ankle in both directions. Repeat with your weight on your right foot.

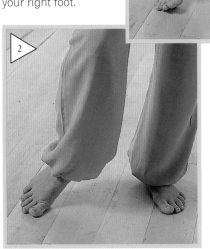

▲ Leg Stretch Stand with your legs apart, hands on your hips. Step forward with your right leg, keeping your left leg straight. Do not bend your knee beyond your front foot. Repeat with your left leg.

➤ **Raising the knee and turning to the side**

Stand with your legs apart, your hands on your hips.
Slowly raise your right leg,
so that your thigh is
parallel to the floor. Turn
your leg out from the hip,
keeping your foot flexed
(sole facing the floor) and
lower your foot. Repeat the
exercise with your left leg.
This is beneficial to your
lower back and will
improve your balance.

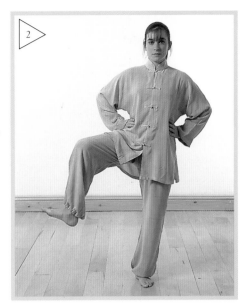

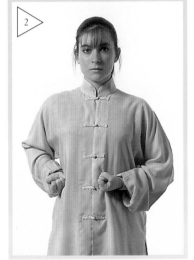

▲ **Tapping the waist to clear
the belt channel** In Chinese
medicine, tapping and rubbing
parts of your body with your hands
and fingers stimulates the healthy
flow of qi around the body. Hold
your fists in front of your body.
Place your right fist on your back
and tap lightly six times, then do
the same with your left fist. Repeat
the sequence starting with your
left fist.

Tai Chi Qigong

*If you believe that health
is a state of mind; then, do
not be deceived, happiness
is a state of the body.
Do not allow your body,
mind and spirit to
squabble, but fuse their
efforts to achieve
your goal.*

Tai Chi Qigong - *Healing Mind*

"THE MIND MOBILIZES the qi; the qi mobilizes the body." Even in the first stages of practice, you will sense the movements of your qi during the qigong exercises. Learn to recognize its flow so that you can direct and store it.

Reservoirs of qi are situated throughout the body, but one of the most important is two inches (5 cm) below your navel in an area called the *dantian* in Chinese. When you practice, the following visualization will help focus your mind:

Imagine that your hips and pelvis are a large sphere on which your upper body rests and from which your legs extend. As you breathe in, the air and qi that you draw in with it fills the sphere; as you breathe out, the air, now carrying toxins and waste products, is expelled, leaving only a few

drops of qi at the very bottom of the sphere. Over time, as you practice tai chi, the sphere will get fuller and heavier, anchoring you to the ground, but without ever weighing you down.

The following 18 tai chi qigong exercises combine the slow, unbroken, rounded movements of the tai chi form with the healing and invigorating action of qigong. They can be performed as individual movements, to concentrate on certain parts of your body, or as a continuous sequence like the tai chi form. If you are performing the exercises singly, you may repeat them from three to six times each. If you wish to perform them as a sequence, follow the instructions given in the introduction to each exercise in the "sequence transition" section.

OPENING THE CHEST

This exercise stimulates your heart-lung function and is beneficial to those suffering from breathing problems, such as asthma.

Sequence transition - *Instead of lowering the arms, keep them at shoulder height, breathe out and straighten the knees. Turn your arms so that the palms of your hands face one another. Bend the elbows and bring the arms toward your chest.*

Go to step 2.

3 Breathe out and bend your knees. If repeating the exercise, lower the arms and straighten your knees.

1 Stand in shoulder-width stance, with your knees slightly bent. Raise your arms to chest height, your palms facing one another.

STARTING POSITION

This exercise will improve your mental functions and adjust the flow of qi in your body.

Stand with your feet shoulder-with apart, toes pointing forward, knees soft. Hold your head and upper back straight, but keep your chest sunk and not stuck out. Your shoulders are relaxed, and your arms hang loosely at your sides. Breathe in and out and visualize the flow of air and qi into your lungs and then down into your dantian.

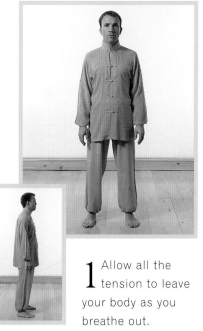

1 Allow all the tension to leave your body as you breathe out.

2 Take a long, slow breath in, and raise your arms to shoulder height. Keep the elbows and wrists soft but do not allow them to flop or hang.

2 Breathe in and separate your arms, opening the chest and straightening your legs.

3 Expand your chest as much as possible as you reach full extension with your arms.

4 Breathe out and bend the knees as you bring the arms back to the center of the body and then lower them.

"*Store up the strength like drawing a bow.
Release the strength like releasing an arrow.*"

WANG ZONYUE

RAINBOW DANCE

This exercise will correct poor posture in your upper back and shoulders by gently stretching your joints and muscles; it will also assist in the prevention and cure of lower-back pain.

Sequence transition - *Instead of dropping your arms all the way down, turn your palms to face one another when your arms are parallel at shoulder-width height. Breathe in and raise your arms over your head.*

Go to step 2.

1 From the starting position stance, raise both hands in the front of your chest. Breathe in, straighten the legs and bring both hands over your head, palms facing each other.

"When the spirit is raised, there is no fault of stagnancy and heaviness."

— WU YUXIANG

2 Shift your weight to your right foot. Raise your left heel off the floor so that only the ball and toes of your left foot are in contact with the floor. Breathe out and turn your body to the right.

3 Breathe in as you bring your left hand down to shoulder height, palm facing up. Your right hand moves up so that your palm is directly over the top of your head.

4 Breathe out, turn to the left and return to the center and reverse the direction of the exercise. It helps to imagine that you are holding a ball between your hand and head.

Separating Clouds By Wheeling Arms

This exercise will prevent arthritis in your knee and shoulder joints. It is also beneficial to your respiratory system.

Sequence transition - *Drawing your feet back to the starting position stance with your weight on both feet, stretch your upper arms in front of you, so both arms are at shoulder height, palms facing up. Bend your knees and lower your arms so that they cross in front of your body, with the left hand over your right.*

Go to step 2.

1 In the starting position stance, cross your arms in front of your body, with your left hand over your right. Breathe out and bend your knees.

2 Breathe in as you raise your arms toward your head, straightening the knees.

6 As you lower your arms, bend your knees slightly.

7 Finish with your arms crossed in front of you.

This movement provides general benefits for the joints and muscles of your upper body and improves your breathing function.

Sequence transition - *Breathe in and stretch your left arm in front of you at chest height, palm facing up, and stretch your right arm behind you. Bend the right elbow, and raise your hand so that it is on the same level as your ear.*

Go to step 2.

3 Open your arms as they rise above your head.

4 Make an arch over your head with your arms, and rotate your palms so that they face outward.

5 Breathe out and begin to lower your arms.

ROLLING ARMS

1 Stand with your left hand stretched out in front of you, palm up, at chest height. Raise your right hand, with your elbow bent, until it is level with your ear.

2 Breathe out as you move your right hand forward and down, simultaneously pulling back your left hand, so that your palms cross in front of your chest.

3 Breathe in as you turn your waist to the left, and shift your weight to your right foot, and stretch out your arms.

4

ROWING THE BOAT IN TH

This exercise is beneficial to the joints of your shoulders, elbows and wrists, and improves your digestive function. It is recommended for those suffering from indigestion, gastritis and other related conditions.

Sequence transition - *After stretching out your arms, turn your waist back to the center and let your arms drop toward you as you breathe out.*

3

4 Breathe out as you draw your hands back so they cross palms facing in front of your chest. Turn your waist to the right and shift your weight to your left foot. Breathe in as you stretch your arms.

1 Stand relaxed in the starting position stance. Breathe in.

LIFTING THE BALL IN FRONT OF THE SHOULDER

In addition to improving your breathing function, this exercise will exercise your shoulder joints, and help any problems with your lower back and neck.

Sequence transition - *Remain in the finishing position of the previous exercise, standing upright and with your arms and legs relaxed.*

During the movement, imagine that you are holding a ball in the palm of your hand.

Go to step 2.

1 Standing in the starting position, stance, raise your right hand, palm facing up, as if holding an imaginary ball.

2 Turn your waist to the left and lift your right foot to your toes, turning it as you shift your weight onto your left foot. Breathe in as you draw you right arm up and across your body.

CENTER OF THE LAKE

2 Bring your arms straight up from the side to the front and around over the top of your head.

3 Breathe out and bend forward as your hands come around and down. Keep your arms straight and your palms facing down.

4 Straighten your body and return to the starting position stance.

PUSHING PALMS WHILE TURNING THE WAIST

3 As you breathe out, turn your right palm face down and lower it naturally. Turn and lower your right foot and return to the starting position. Repeat the whole movement with your left arm.

This dynamic qi-generating movement is particularly beneficial to the spine, and is recommended for people who suffer from lower-back problems.

Sequence transition - *Lower your foot and turn your waist back to the center. Draw your left arm back to your waist, shift your weight onto your left foot, turn your waist to the left and push forward with your right palm.*

Go to step 2.

1 Stand in the starting position stance and hold your hands at your waist, palms up. Draw back your left hand, turn your waist to the left and push forward with your right palm.

2 Breathe in. Draw the right hand back as you move your weight back to the center. Your palms cross facing one other.

3 Shift your weight to the right foot and turn your waist to the right. Breathe out as your left palm pushes forward.

LOOKING A

3 Turn your waist to the right; bringing your right hand in front of your face, and drop your left hand across your body.

4 In effect, you are drawing two linked circles in front of you with your hands as you shift your weight from on foot to the other.

The turning motion of this exercise is beneficial to the entire spinal area, from the lower-back to the neck.

Sequence transition - *As you allow your weight to settle in the center, lower your arms to your sides and relax the shoulders, elbows and wrists.*

Unless otherwise stated in the instructions, during the qigong exercises, your fingers should be extended in a natural curve and not stretched or held in a fist. Keep the thumb in line with your fingers.

CLOUD HANDS IN HORSE STANCE

This exercise will improve your mental and breathing functions. It is recommended for those with shoulder and low-back problems.

Sequence transition - *Allow your arms to drop slowly to your sides as you shift your weight to the center so that you are supported equally by both feet. Bend your knees and raise both hands to your waist. This position is called horse stance.*

In the horse stance, your weight is evenly distributed between both feet, shoulder-width apart, and your knees bent, as if sitting astride a horse.

1 Stand in horse stance (see left). Raise your left hand, palm facing you, level with your head, and bring your right hand, palm facing you, to waist height.

2 Turn your waist to the left. Lower your left hand, and raise your right hand, palm facing upward.

THE MOON BY TURNING THE BODY

1 Stand with your arms at your sides. Turn your body to the left, shifting your weight to your left foot, and bringing your right foot to its toes. Breathe in as you swing both arms up.

2 Allow your right elbow to bend, right palm facing up, and the left facing down. Breathe out as you bend your knees, turn your waist to the center and lower your arms.

3 Repeat the movement turning to the right, breathing in as your body rises and out as its lowers.

PUNCHING IN HORSE STANCE

This exercise, borrowed from "hard" kung fu styles, such as karate, is used in tai chi to develop internal as well as external strength.

Sequence transition - *Lower the arms, turn the waist to the center. Draw your arms to waist height, elbows bent, hands held in soft fists. Bend your knees and adopt the horse stance. Raise your fists to waist height.*

1 Stand in the horse stance, with your hands at your sides, in fists at waist height. Punch with your right arm, twisting the fist so that it finishes palm down.

2 Breathe out as you pull back your right hand and prepare to punch with your left hand. Breathe in as your fist completes the punch.

SCOOPING THE SEA WHILE LOOKING AT THE SKY

The forward and backward bending movements of this exercise are beneficial to the spine, and massage the internal organs, promoting their health and the flow of qi that ensures their proper functioning.

Sequence transition - *Open your hands and stretch both arms in front of you. Take a bow step with your left foot.*

Left bow step: Step out to the left with your left foot, toes pointing out, and shift your weight onto it. Your right knee remains straight and the right toes point forward.

3

1 From the starting position stance, take a bow step to the left (see left for description) and stretch your arms in front of you.

2 Lean forward, bringing both hands together in front of your left knee. Bend your left knee further but do not allow it to go over the toes of your left foot.

"*When the left side is heavy, it empties, and the right side is already countering. The qi is like a wheel, and the whole body must coordinate.*"

— LI YIYU

A good exercise for the joints of the entire body, which will also improve your coordination. This extremely relaxing movement is beneficial to your mental functions.

Sequence transition - *Remain in the right bow stance (see previous exercise), shift your weight back so you are supported by both feet, and draw your arms to the side of your body, palms facing out.*

Go to step 2.

3 As you begin to shift your weight from your left to your right foot, draw your arms back and open them.

4 Breathe in and look up as you open your arms wide. Return to the starting position stance and repeat taking a right bow step.

FLYING PIGEON

This exercise regulates the respiratory, digestive and circulatory functions. Sufferers from breathing problems, such as bronchitis and emphysema, will benefit from this movement.

Sequence transition - *Shift your weight to your right foot, move your left foot to the right, toes pointing forward. Lift your arms to your side.*

Go to step 2.

1 Step forward with your left foot, lift up both arms to the side. Breathe in and put your weight on your right foot and lift up the toes of the left foot.

2 Breathe out and transfer your weight to your left foot, raising the heel of your right foot as you bring your hands together in front of your chest.

PUSHING WAVE

1 Step into the bow stance (see page 34) with your left foot. Lift your hands to your sides, palms facing out.

2 Put your weight onto your left foot and push forward with your hands. Breathe out and stretch the back leg and lift your right heel off the floor.

3 Slowly move your weight to your right leg. Breathe in and pull your arms back. Repeat the movement with a right bow stance.

FLYING WILD GOOSE

This exercise is recommended to relax after a stressful day; it will also improve your respiratory function.

Sequence transition - *Lower your arms to your sides and step forward so that you are standing in horse stance. Draw your arms slightly away from your body, but keep them relaxed, with the joints soft and rounded.*

Go to step 2.

3 Pull back and repeat the exercise stepping forward with your right foot.

1 Stand in horse stance (see page 33), with your arms slightly apart from your sides, palms facing in.

1

2 Breathe in as you straighten your knees and raise both arms to the side.

3 Stretch your hands in line with your arms. and begin to sink down.

4 Breathe out as your hands drop and your knees bend.

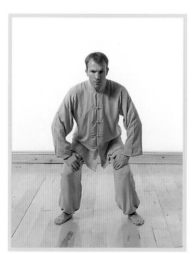

3 Rotate your body from your waist to the left until you have completed one full circle.

4 Breathe in as you rise to complete the circle. Keep your shoulders and back relaxed during the movement.

5 Return to the center and repeat the circling motion to the right.

ROTATING WHEEL IN A CIRCLE

This exercise is beneficial to the spine and will help sufferers of low-back problems.

Sequence transition - *Continue to bend your knees until you are in a crouching position. Support the weight of your upper body with your hands on your thighs, fingers pointing inward.*

Go to step 3.

1 Stand with you feet slightly wider than shoulder width, with your arms by your sides.

2 Breathe out and bend forward, supporting your weight with your hands resting on your thighs. Your fingers should point inward.

MARCHING WHILE BOUNCING BALL

This exercises strengthens many of the internal organs and can be used in cases of indigestion and other digestive problems and tiredness, as well as problems with your sexual function.

Sequence transition - *Straighten your knees, and raise your right foot by bending your knee, and lift your left hand to shoulder height, palm facing forward.*

Go to step 2.

1 Raise your right foot, toes relaxed, and lift your left hand to shoulder height, palm forward.

2 Breathe out and imagine you are bouncing a ball, as you lower your leg and hand.

3 ▷

SHAU GONG (BALANCING QI)

The concluding exercise in the sequence will balance the flow of qi in your body. It is also recommended for ailments of the digestive system.

Sequence transition - *lower your arm and leg. Breathe in and turn your arms to the side, palms facing up.*

Follow instruction 2.

3 Breathe in as you raise your left leg and right arm, bouncing the ball with your left hand.

1 Stand in the starting position stance. Breathe in and raise your arms to the side, palms facing upward.

2 When your arms are above your head, your palms face downward, in front of your head.

3 Breathe out and lower your arms along the front of your body.

4 Bring your arms down to your stomach. Keep the shoulders, elbows and wrists soft and rounded.

"*The motion should be rooted in the feet, released through the legs, controlled by the waist, and manifested through the fingers.*"

- ZHANG SANFENG

Six-Method Qigong

He who believes that life is a race will lose it; he who believes that happiness makes the earth stand still will run out of time.

Six-method Qigong

DO NOT BE disheartened if there are days when work or family responsibilities prevent you from completing the full warm-up and tai chi qigong sequence. But rather than doing no tai chi practice at all, perform, without rushing them, as many of the tai chi qigong exercises as is possible in the time available to you. Alternatively, you may use the six-method qigong, which provides a short, comprehensive sequence of exercises to increase and regulate your qi.

GATHERING THE QI

1 Stand with your right foot at right angles to your left foot, with both knees slightly bent. Rest your left hand on your hip, and hold your right hand below your navel, palm facing up.

2 Turn to the right from the waist (and not the shoulders) and raise your hand upward and outward in a broad arc.

3 Breathe in and straighten your knees, until your right hand reaches head height, palm facing you.

4 On the out breath, turn your waist to the center, lower your right hand down the center of your body and bend your knees.

5 As you breathe in, imagine that you are drawing the qi into your hand. You may notice it change color and heat up. When you breathe out, draw the qi down along the center of the body. Repeat three to six times.

CRANE SIPS THE WATER

"Let the qi move without breaks so that there is no part it cannot reach."

— WU YUXIANG

1 Stand with your weight on your right leg and bend your knees. Hold both hands at in front of you, palms down.

2 Breathe out and slide your left foot, heel first, along the floor.

3 Breathe in, raise your left foot off the floor and lift your arms slightly.

4 Lift your foot higher by bending your left knee until your thigh is at right angle to your body.

5 Return to the starting position and repeat the exercise with your weight resting on your left leg.

WHITE CRANE SPREADS ITS WINGS

1 Stand with your feet slightly apart. Raise your arms to the side, fingers, soft, hanging down.

2 Breathe in and continue raising your arms to shoulder height. Keep the fingers relaxed.

3 Raise your hands so your fingers point upward, breathe out and bend the knees.

4 As you sink into the floor on bent knees, lower your arms, stretching your elbows and wrists.

5 When your arms are at your sides, your palms should face inward. As you breathe in and out, imagine that the qi is flowing to and from your hands through your palms.

CASTING THE FISHING NET

Stand with your legs apart, knees slightly bent, with your left (rear) foot at right angles to your right (front) foot. Hold your hands in front of you, palms down, keeping your shoulders relaxed and your elbows soft. Shift your weight from your front to your rear foot. Then turn your waist in time with the forward and backward movement.

DRAGON CHASES THE MOON

In the same stance as the previous exercise, shift your weight forward and backward from your front to your rear foot. With your shoulders, elbows and wrists rounded and soft, circle both hands in a clockwise direction so that they cross in the center of the body.

DRAGON SWIMMING (TRIPLE RINGS)

1 Stand with your feet and legs together. Press your palms together at chest height.

2 Raise your arms to the left, while twisting your legs and body to follow your hands.

3 Make a circle above your head with your hands leading your body to the right.

4 After circling your head, bend your knees and make a second circle to the left at chest height.

"*If the body is clumsy, then in advancing or retreating it cannot be free.*"

- LI YIYU

5 Twist the arms around so that the right arm remains lower than the left.

6 Bend your knees as you start the third and final circle at waist height. Twist to the right.

7 The final circle follows in the same direction, with your left arm uppermost.

8 Double back to the center of your body and complete the final ring.

9 Move slowly and breathe evenly as you lower your body to the lowest point.

10 Repeat the three circles from your waist up in the opposite direction.

11 Finish with your legs straight and your hands clasped over your head.

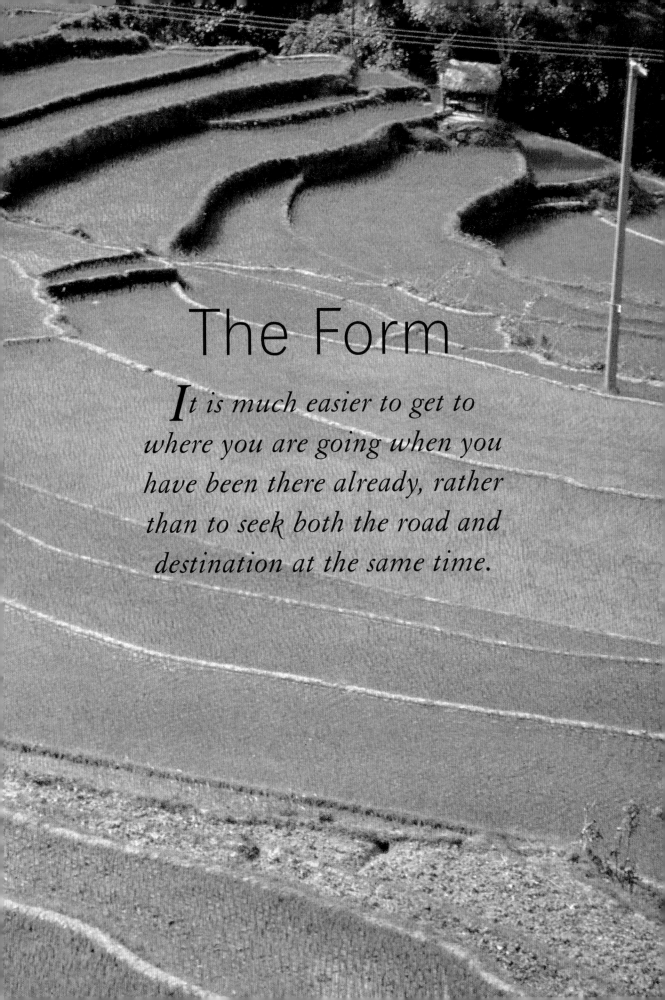

The Form

It is much easier to get to where you are going when you have been there already, rather than to seek both the road and destination at the same time.

Twenty-Four Step
Simplified Tai Chi Chuan

ON THE SURFACE the form appears to be no more than a sequence of punches, kicks and parrys, which are common to many of the martial arts; but at a deeper level, the correct practice of the form requires an understanding of breathing techniques, of the circulation of qi, and of the focused one-pointed mind of meditation.

Many students are discouraged in the early stages of practice, because there seem to be so many elements to remember for each step. But you will quickly discover that many of the 24 steps are composed of shared movements of the feet, hands and waist. Approach your study of the form in stages. Learn and practice the main steps of the first three postures, and then the transitions that link them. It is much easier to go from A to B when you have been to B already, rather than looking for both the way and destination at the same time. When you have learned the first three steps, add another three, and so on, until you have covered the full 24. Then you may concentrate on the other aspects of the form, such as breathing and the circulation of qi.

To help you work out which way you should be facing, imagine that you are standing in the center of a clock face, looking toward 12 o'clock at the beginning of the form, with 3 o'clock on your right, and 9 o'clock on your left.

① COMMENCING FORM

1 Facing 12 o'clock, stand with your feet shoulder-width apart, toes pointing forward, knees relaxed. Your arms hang by your sides, fingers and thumb in alignment and slightly curved.

2 Breathe in and raise your arms, palms facing down, to shoulder height. Hold your mind in your *dantian* and imagine the flow of qi into your lungs as you draw in the air.

3 Your shoulders and elbows are soft and your head straight as you breathe out. Press your palms down and bend your knees. Keep your chest sunken and pull in your seat.

4 Continue to lower your hands, palms down, until they are at hip height. Your weight should be equally distributed on both your feet. Keep your knees bent, unless otherwise instructed.

② PART WILD HORSE MANE ON BOTH

5 Turn to the right (to 1 o'clock) and shift your weight onto your right foot. Raise your right hand, palm down, to shoulder height.

6 Move your left hand, palm up, under your right hand, as if you were holding a ball in front of you. This is known as the "hold-ball" gesture. Look at your right hand.

9 Shift your weight onto your left (leading) foot. Raise your left hand to eye level, with the palm facing up, and lower your right hand to your hip, with your palm facing down. You are facing 9 o'clock.

10 Move your weight back onto your right foot. Raise the toes of your left foot and turn them out (left) before putting your foot flat on the floor.

SIDES

7 Lift your left foot and bring it next to your right foot, with your left heel off the floor.

8 Turn your body to the left and step into a left bow stance (see page 34 for detailed explanation) so your body faces 8 o'clock. When you step, put your left heel down first. Begin to push your left hand up, and to press your right hand down.

11 Shift your weight onto your left foot, and draw your hands into a hold-ball gesture in front of your left side with your left arm uppermost.

12 Complete the hold-ball gesture. Draw your right foot next to your left foot, with only your right toes on the floor. Look at your left hand.

13 ▷

13 Move your weight back onto your left foot. Turn to the right and step with your right foot to 10:30.

14 Complete the right bow stance, turning your right toes out before putting them down. Raise your right hand to eye level, and press your left hand down by your left hip. Look at your right hand. You are facing 9 o'clock.

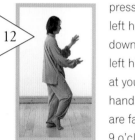

15 Shift your weight onto your left foot and sit back, raising the toes of your right foot off the floor and turning them out slightly.

16 Put your right foot down and shift your weight onto it. Draw your left foot next to your right foot, and make a hold-ball gesture in front of you on the right side of your body, with your right arm on top. Look at your right hand.

You breathe in as your body rises and expands, and breathe out as it lowers and contracts.

17 The sequence then follows the same steps as the first part of the horse mane.

18 Shift your weight to your right foot, raising your left toes off the floor and sit back. Turn your body to the left and take a left bow step (to 8 o'clock).

❸ WHITE CRANE SPREADS ITS WINGS

20 Shift all your weight onto you left foot. Turn to the left and make a hold-ball gesture in front of your left side, with the left hand on top. Look at your left hand.

21 Draw your right foot behind your left foot. Turn slightly to the right and look at your right hand. Sit back onto your right foot.

The parting the mane action occurs three times in all. Hold your upper body upright, as if your head were suspended by a thread, and keep your chest sunk. Your arm movements should be large and rounded. When you turn your body, turn from your waist, and not from your shoulders. When you step forward, put your foot down slowly in position, with the heel touching first. Your leading knee should not go beyond the toes of your leading foot, and your rear foot should be at a 45–60° angle to your front foot.

19 Part the horse's mane for the third and final time, completing the left bow step to 8 o'clock, with your left hand raised at eye level and your right hand down by your right hip. Look straight ahead, toward 9 o'clock.

Do not stick your chest out. Your arms should be rounded when they move up or down. You should raise your right hand as you shift your weight back onto your right leg. Your left foot carries no weight, and your left knee is slightly bent.

22 Move your left foot forward and rest on its toes, but without shifting any weight onto it. This is called an "empty stance." Turn slightly to the left, and raise your right hand forward until it is level with your right temple, palm facing in. Your left hand lowers until it stops, palm down, in front of your left hip. Look straight ahead to 9 o'clock.

23

④ BRUSH KNEE AND TWIST STEP ON

23 Remain in the empty stance and turn left to 8 o'clock. Your right hand moves down and your left hand up.

24 Turn to the right, your right hand moving down, palm up, past your face, while your left hand, palm down circles up, stopping in front of your right side.

27 Complete the bow stance and stop your left hand beside your left hip, palm down. Look at the fingers of your extended right hand, palm out.

28 Shift your weight to your right foot, bending your right knee. Raise the toes of your left foot and turn them slightly out (left) before placing your foot flat on floor.

BOTH SIDES

25 Turn to the left. prepare to take a left bow step to 8 o'clock. Draw your right hand left past your right ear.

26 After you turn your body, push your right hand forward at nose level, palm facing out, while your left hand drops and circles around your left knee.

29 Bend your left leg. Turn your body to the left and shift your weight onto your left foot.

30 Bring your right foot next to your left foot, resting it on its toes. Move your left hand, palm tilted up, to shoulder height, while your right hand, as your body turns, curves up and down to the left, stopping in front of your left side, palm tilted down. Look at your left hand.

31

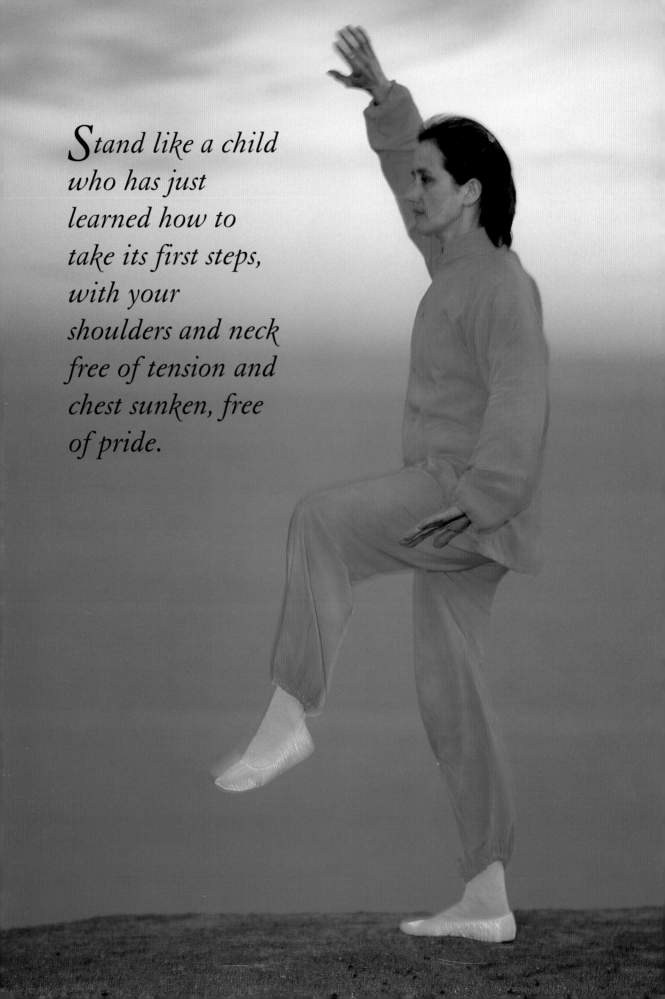

Stand like a child who has just learned how to take its first steps, with your shoulders and neck free of tension and chest sunken, free of pride.

31 Take a right bow step to 10 o'clock. Draw your left hand past your left ear.

32 After you turn your body, push your left hand forward at nose level, palm facing out, while your right hand drops and circles around your right knee to stop beside your right hip. Look at your left hand (to 9 o'clock).

33 Shift your weight to your left foot, bending your left knee. Raise the toes of your right foot and turn them slightly out (right) before placing your foot flat on floor.

34 Bend your right leg. Turn to the right and shift your weight to your right foot. Move your left hand across your face and circle your right hand out and back to your ear.

35 Make a left bow stance (to 8 o'clock) and circle your left hand down and stop by your left hip, palm facing down. Push the right hand until the arm is extended. Look at the fingers of your right hand, palm facing out. You are facing 9 o'clock at the close of the movement.

6 STEP BACK

38 Complete the left empty stance by resting your left foot on its heel, but without shifting any weight onto it. Do not rise or fall as you move into the final position. Look at your left hand. You are facing 9 o'clock.

39 Turn slightly to the right. Lower your right hand, palm facing up, toward your hip in a circular motion.

⑤ HAND STRUMS THE LUTE

36 Take half a step with your right foot toward your left heel. Turn to the right slightly, and shift your weight onto your right foot.

37 As you turn raise your left hand to nose level, palm facing right, elbow slightly bent. Circle your right hand opposite your left elbow, palm facing left. Raise your left foot.

TO DRIVE MONKEY AWAY

40 Continue circling your right hand until it reaches shoulder level with your palm facing up and your elbow slightly bent.

41 Bring your right hand toward your right ear, and turn to the left. Push your right hand forward and your left hand down by your waist as you raise your left foot to step back.

42

42 Place your left foot in position on the floor from toes to heel. Turn your body to the left and shift your weight onto your left foot to make a right empty stance, with your right foot pivoting on its toes until it points forward. Look at your right hand (to 9 o'clock).

45 Turn slightly to the right. Lower your right hand toward your hip in a circular motion.

46 Continue circling your right hand until it reaches shoulder level with your palm facing up and your elbow slightly bent.

43 Bring your left hand level with your left ear and turn to the right. Push your left hand forward.

44 As your hands move, raise your right foot and step back as before, this time shifting your weight to the right foot. Look at your left hand (to 9 o'clock).

47 Bring your right hand toward your right ear, and turn to the left. Push your right hand forward and the left down by your waist as you step back with your left foot.

48 Place your foot slowly in position, from toes to heel. Turn your body to the left and shift your weight onto your left foot to form an empty step. Look at your right hand (to 9 o'clock).

49

49 Bring your left hand level with your ear and turn to the right. Push your left hand forward.

50 As your hands move, raise your right foot and step back as before, this time shifting your weight to the right foot.

⑦ GRASP THE BIRD'S TAIL–LEFT STYLE

52 Turn to the right. Move your right hand up and to the side, to shoulder height, palm facing up, while your left hand is palm down. Look at your left hand.

53 Make a hold-ball in front of your right side, with your right hand on top. Shift your weight onto your right foot, draw your left foot, on its toes, next to your right foot. Look at your right hand (to 11 o'clock).

51 Bring your left hand level with your ear and turn to the right. Push your left hand forward.

54 Turn your body slightly to the left, raise your left foot and step forward.

55 Turn a little more to the left (so that you are facing 9 o'clock), and complete the left bow stance. Push out your left forearm, palm facing in. Drop your right hand by your right hip, palm down, fingers pointing forward. Look at your left forearm.

56 ▷

Move through the form at a constant pace, as if your were swimming on dry land, your limbs and head buoyed up by the universal qi.

56 Sit back, shifting you weight onto your right foot. Turn to the left, while stretching your left hand forward, palm down. Bring your right hand up, palm turning upward, until it is below your left forearm.

57 Turn to the right, while drawing your hands in an arc in front of you, finishing with your right hand extended to the side at shoulder height, palm up, and the left forearm across your chest, palm in. Shift your weight onto the right foot. Look at your right hand.

58 Turn slightly to the left. Bend your right arm and place your right hand inside your left wrist.

59

59 Turn a little farther to the left. Press both hands forward, with your right palm facing out and your left palm facing in. Keep your left arm rounded. Shift your weight slowly onto your left foot to make a left bow stance. Look at your left wrist (to 9 o'clock).

62 Lower both your hands to your waist. Do not lower them in a straight line, but in an S-shaped movement.

63 Shift your weight onto your left foot, making a left bow stance. Push your hands forward and up (but curving up and not in a diagonal line), palms facing forward, until your wrists are at shoulder height. You are facing 9 o'clock.

60 Turn both palms down as your right hand passes over your left wrist and moves forward and to the right, ending level with your left hand.

61 Open your hands shoulder-width apart, and shift your weight onto your right foot, left toes lifted. Pull back your hands in front of you, palms facing out and slightly down. Look straight ahead (to 9 o'clock).

⑧ GRASP THE BIRD'S TAIL–RIGHT STYLE

64 Sit back, shifting your weight onto your right foot, and lift your left toes.

65 Turn to the right and pivot the toes of your left foot in. Move your right arm to the right. Turn the left palm out.

66 ▷

66 Move your right hand past your abdomen, and up to your left ribs, palm up, forming a hold-ball gesture with your left hand on top. Shift your weight back onto your left foot.

67 Place your right foot beside your left foot, with its heel raised. Look at your left hand.

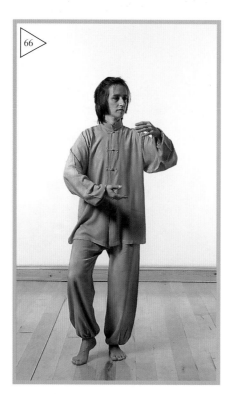

70 Turn to the right, stretching your right hand, palm down. Raise your left hand, palm turning up, until it is below your right forearm.

71 Turn to the left. Draw your hands in an arc, so your left hand is at shoulder height, palm up, and your right forearm across your chest, palm in. Shift your weight onto your left foot. Look at your left hand.

68 Turn to the right (to 3 o'clock). Take a step to the right (4 o'clock) with your right foot, placing your foot down heel first.

69 Complete the right bow stance, shifting your weight onto your right leg. Push out your right forearm, palm facing in. Drop your left hand by your left hip, palm down, fingers pointing forward. Look at your right forearm (to 3 o'clock).

72 Turn slightly to the right. Bend your left arm and place your left hand inside your right wrist.

73 Turn a little farther to the right. Press both hands forward, with your left palm facing out and your right palm facing in; your right arm is rounded. Shift your weight onto your right foot to take a right bow stance. Look at your right wrist (to 3 o'clock).

74

74 Turn both your palms down as your left hand passes over your right wrist and moves forward and to the left, ending level with your right hand.

75 Open your hands shoulder-width apart, palms turning out and down. Sit back onto your left foot, with your right toes raised off the floor.

⑨ SINGLE WHIP

78 Sit back and shift your weight onto your left foot and turn in the toes of your right foot.

79 Turn your body to the left. Move your hands left, with your left hand on top, until your left arm is stretched at shoulder height, palm facing out, and your right hand is in front of your left ribs, palm tilted in. Look at your left hand (to 10 o'clock).

76 Draw your palms down from chest to waist height.

77 Shift your weight onto your right foot, making a right bow stance. Push your hands forward and up, palms facing forward until your wrists are at shoulder height. You are facing 3 o'clock in the final position.

80 Turn your body to the right, shifting your weight onto your right foot. Draw your left foot on its toes next to your right foot. Make an arc up and round to the right with your right hand until your arm is at shoulder height.

81 With the right palm turned out, bunch your fingertips and turn them down from the wrist to form a "hooked hand."

82

82 Turn your body to the left, facing 9 o'clock, and take a step forward with your left foot (to 8 o'clock), heel first.

83 Your left arm moves left at eye level, the palm turning out as it sweeps across. Step into a left bow stance. Look at your left hand (to 9 o'clock).

85 At the same time, open your hooked right hand and turn the palm out. Look at your right hand (to 3 o'clock).

86 Turn to the left, shifting your weight onto your left foot. Make an arc past your face with your left hand, turning your left palm out. Look at your left hand.

⑩ WAVE HANDS LIKE CLOUDS—LEFT STYLE

84 Shift your weight onto your right foot and turn your body to the right, turning the toes of your left foot in. Make an arc with the left hand, past your abdomen and finishing in front of your right shoulder, palm tilted in.

87 Your right hand makes an arc past your abdomen and then up to your left shoulder, with the palm tilted in.

88 Bring your right foot next to your left foot, so that your feet are in parallel stance, and about 4–8 in. (10–20 cm) apart.

89 ▷

Practice the form in the open spaces of nature — a clearing amid the trees, or at the foot of a hill, where the earth qi is carried down to you.

89 Turn to the right and shift your weight onto your right foot. Look at your right hand (to 3 o'clock).

90 Your right hand continues to move right, past your face, palm turned out, while your left hand makes an arc past your abdomen and up to shoulder level, with the palm tilted in. Then take a side step with your left foot. Look at your left hand.

91 Shift your weight onto your right foot and turn your body to the right, while turning the toes of your left foot in. Make an arc with your left hand.

92 Turn to the left, shifting your weight onto your left foot. Make an arc past your face with your left hand, turning your left palm out.

93

93 Your right hand makes an arc past your abdomen and then up to your left shoulder, with the palm tilted in.

94 Bring your right foot to the side of your left foot, so that your feet are in parallel stance, about 4–8 in. (10–20 cm) apart. Look at your right hand.

96 Turn your body to the left, facing 9 o'clock, and take a step forward with your left foot, heel touching the floor first, (to 8 o'clock).

97 Slowly rotate your left palm and push your left arm ahead at eye level. Start shifting your weight onto your left foot.

⑪ SINGLE WHIP

POINTS TO REMEMBER

Your lower spine serves as the axis for the body turns. Keep your waist and hips relaxed and avoid a sudden rise or fall of body position. The movement of your arms should be relaxed and circular, and follow that of the waist. The pace must be slow and even. Keep your balance when moving your lower limbs. Follow the hand with your eyes when it moves past your face.

95 Turn to the right. At the same time, move the right hand toward the right side and form a hooked hand at a point slightly above shoulder height, while your left hand makes an arc past your abdomen and up to your right shoulder, with your left palm turned in.

POINTS TO REMEMBER

Keep your upper body straight and your waist relaxed. Bend your right elbow slightly down and have your left elbow directly above your left knee. Lower your shoulders. Turn out your left palm in time as you press your left hand forward.

98 Complete the left bow stance. Look at your left hand (to 9 o'clock).

▷ 99

⑫ HIGH PAT ON HORSE

99 Take half a step forward with your right foot and shift your weight onto it. Open your right hook hand and turn both palms up, elbows slightly bent, while you turn slightly to the right, raising the left heel. Look ahead. Turn to the left (to 9 o'clock).

100 Draw your right hand past your right ear and push it

102 Separate your hands, each making a downward circle with the palms tilted down. Raise your left foot to take a step forward (to 8 o'clock).

103 Place your left foot down to make a left bow stance, with your left toes slightly turned out. Look straight ahead. Continue to circle your hands out.

⓭ KICK WITH RIGHT HEEL

100 continued: forward, palm out, at eye level. Lower your left hand until it comes in front of your left hip, palm up. Bring your left foot forward, forming an empty stance. Look at your right hand.

101 With your weight supported on your right foot, turn to the right (to 10 o'clock), and cross your left hand, palm in, over your right wrist, palm out.

104 Bring your hands up until they cross in front of your chest, with your left hand over your right hand, palms in.

105 Open your arms to the side at shoulder height, with your elbows bent and your palms turning out. Raise your right leg, bent at knee, and kick with your right foot (to 10 o'clock). Your right arm is over the right leg. Look at your right hand.

(14) STRIKE WITH BOTH FISTS

106 Pull back your right foot but keep your thigh parallel to the floor. Move your left hand up and forward, then down to the side of your right hand in front of your chest, turning both palms up.

107 Both arms, elbows soft, drop to either side of your right knee. Look straight ahead.

(15) TURN AND

109 Extend your fists up, as if you were punching someone on both ears, with the knuckles tilted up. The distance between your fists is about 4–8 in. (10–20 cm). Look between your fists.

110 Bend your left leg and sit back. Turn your body to the left, with the toes of your right foot pointing in. Open your hands and move them out and down.

POINTS TO REMEMBER

Hold your head and neck straight. Your fists are loosely clenched. Keep your shoulders relaxed, and allow your arms to move down naturally with your elbows slightly bent.

108 Put down your right foot, slightly to the right and forward of your left foot (to 10 o'clock). Shift your weight onto your right foot to make a bow step. Drop both hands and clench the fists loosely.

KICK WITH LEFT HEEL

111 Continue to separate your hands, palms facing forward, in a circular movement. Straightening your arms at the elbow, look at your left hand.

112 Shift your weight onto your right foot. Bring your left next to it and rest its toes, and circle your hands downward and to the sides.

113 Continue circling in and forward, until your hands cross in front of your chest, with your right hand over your left hand, both palms facing in. Look ahead.

114 Raise your left foot off the floor and start to separate your hands to the side.

115 Open your arms to the side at shoulder level, elbows slightly bent and palms turning out. Kick with your left heel (to 4 o'clock), and look at your left hand.

POINTS TO REMEMBER

As in the right style, your wrists are level with your shoulders when you open your hands. Your right leg is slightly bent when your left foot kicks; the force of the kick comes from your heel, with the upturned toes pointing slightly in. Coordinate the separation of your hands with the kick. The left arm is parallel with the left leg.

116

Your attention resides in your dantian throughout the form, so that your movements issue from your center and radiate out to your head and limbs.

⑯ SQUAT DOWN AND STAND ON ONE LEG

116 Pull back your left foot but keep it raised, with your thigh parallel to the floor.

117 Turn to the right. Make a right hooked hand. Your left palm turns up and makes an arc across your body until it is in front of your right shoulder, tilted in. Look at your right hand.

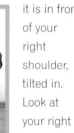

120 Using your heel as a pivot, turn the toes of your left foot slightly out so that they come in line with your outstretched leg; turn the toes of your right foot in, as your right leg straightens and your left leg bends. Your weight is shifted onto your left foot. Your body turns slightly to the left and then rises in a forward movement (to 3 o'clock). Your left arm continues to extend forward, with the palm facing the right side,

POINTS TO REMEMBER

Raise your left foot slightly before crouching and stretching your left leg. Bend your standing leg slightly. Your toes should point naturally down as your raise your right foot.

120 continued: while the right hand drops behind the back, with bunched fingertips pointing backward. Look at your left hand.

– LEFT STYLE

118 Turn to the left (to 3 o'clock and bend your right knee, stretching your left leg to the side (to 2 o'clock). Extend your left hand along the inner side of your left leg, palm facing forward. Look at your left hand.

119 When your right leg is bent in a full crouch, turn the toes of your right foot out slightly and straighten your left leg with the toes turned in slightly.

121 Raise your right foot until your right thigh is parallel to the floor.

122 Open your right hand and swing it outside your right leg and then up to the front, until your bent right elbow is just above your right knee, fingers pointing up and palm facing left. Lower your left hand to your hip, palm facing down. Look at your right hand (to 3 o'clock).

123

⑰ SQUAT DOWN AND STAND ON ONE LEG

123 Put your right foot down on its toes in front of your left foot, and shift your weight onto it. Turn your body to the left, using the ball of your left toes as a pivot.

124 Raise your left hand to the side to shoulder height and make a left hooked hand.

127 When your left leg is fully bent, turn the toes of your left foot out and straighten your right leg with the toes turned in.

128 Turn the toes of your right foot slightly out, in line with your outstretched leg; turn the toes of your left foot in as your left leg straightens and your right leg bends. Shift your weight onto your right foot. Your body turns slightly to the right and then rise in a forward movement. Your right

— RIGHT STYLE

125 Your right hand, following the body turn, moves in an arc until it comes in front of your left shoulder with the fingers pointing up. Look at your left hand (to 11 o'clock).

126 Bend your left knee, stretching your right leg to the side (to 4 o'clock). Extend your right hand along your inner right leg, palm facing forward. Look at your right hand.

POINTS TO REMEMBER

Raise your right foot slightly before crouching and stretching your right leg. Bend the standing leg slightly. The toes should point naturally down as your raise your left foot.

128 continued: arm continues to stretch forward, with the palm facing left, while your left hand drops behind your back, with bunched fingertips pointing backward. Look at your right hand.

129 Begin to raise your left foot until your thigh is parallel to the floor.

130 Open your left hand and swing it past your left leg and up, until your bent elbow is above your left knee, fingers pointing up. Lower your right hand to your hip, palm down. Look at your left hand.

131 Turn to the left (to 1 o'clock). Put your left foot down, toes pointing out. Bend your knees. Make a hold-ball gesture with the left hand on top.

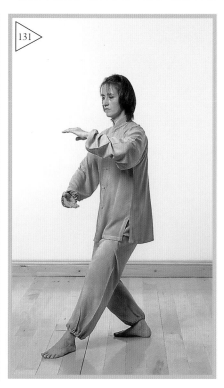

134 Complete the right bow stance.

135 Move your right hand up, stopping just above your right temple, with your palm tilted up. Move your left hand down to the left side, and then push it forward and up to nose level, with the palm facing forward. Look at your left hand.

WORKS SHUTTLES

132 Shift your weight to your left foot, and move your right foot, on its toes, next to your left foot. Look at the left forearm.

133 Sit back on your left foot and take a step with your right foot (to 4 o'clock).

136 Turn slightly to the right, shifting your weight back, with the toes of your right foot turned out. Make a hold-ball gesture with the right hand on top. Look at your right forearm.

137 Shift your weight onto your right foot and place your left foot next to it with the heel raised and the toes on the floor.

138

138 Turn to the left and take a step to 2 o'clock with the left foot, placing your heel down first.

⑲ NEEDLE AT SEA BOTTOM

141 Take half a step forward with your right foot. Shift your weight onto your right foot as your left foot moves forward to form a left empty stance. Turn your body to the right (to 4 o'clock).

142 Lower your right hand, then raise it up to the side of your right ear and, with the body turning to 3 o'clock, thrust it down in front of your body, with the palm facing left and the

139 Shift your weight onto your left foot to complete the left bow stance.

140 Move your left hand up, stopping just above your left temple, with the palm tilted up. Move your right hand down to the right side, and then push it forward and up to nose level, with the palm facing forward. Look at your right hand.

㉗ FAN PENETRATES BACK

143 Turn slightly to the right. Make a left bow step forward. At the same time, raise your right arm with your elbow bent until your right hand stops just above your right temple.

142 continued:
fingers pointing down. Make an arc with your left hand forward and down to the side of your left hip, palm facing down and fingers pointing forward. Look down.

144

144 Complete the bow

stance. Tilt the palm up with the thumb pointing down. Raise your left hand slightly and push it forward at nose level, palm facing forward. Look at your left hand (to 2 o'clock). The distance between your heels should be about 4 in. (10 cm).

POINTS TO REMEMBER

Keep your upper body erect, and relax your waist and hips as well as the muscles in your back. Coordinate the movement of your left leg with that of your left arm.

146 continued: knuckles turned down. Lower your left hand to the side of your left hip, with the palm turned downward and the fingers pointing forward. At the same time, draw back your right foot and, without stopping or allowing it to touch floor, take a step to 10 o'clock with the toes turned out. Look at your right fist.

147 Shift your weight onto

your right foot. Move your left hand up and forward from the left

POINTS TO REMEMBER

Clench your right fist loosely. While pulling back your fist, your forearm is first turned in and then out. While the fist strikes forward, your right shoulder follows the movement and extends slightly forward. Hold your shoulder and elbows down.

147 continued: side in a circular movement, palm turned slightly down, and pull the right fist in back to the right side of the waist, knuckles turned down.

㉑ TURN, DEFLECT DOWNWARD, PARRY AND PUNCH

145 Shift your weight onto your right foot, turn to the right, and shift your weight back onto your left foot. Face 6 o'clock. As you turn, circle your right hand toward the right and down. Make a fist and move it to your left side, knuckles up. Raise your left arm above your head, with the palm tilted up. Look forward.

146 Turn your body to the right. Thrust your right fist up and forward in front of your chest,

148 Take a step forward with your left foot. Look at your left hand (to 9 o'clock).

149 Complete the left bow stance and strike forward with your right fist at chest height, with the back of the hand facing the right side. Pull your left hand back to the side of the right forearm. Look at your right fist (to 9 o'clock).

150

㉒ WITHDRAW AND PUSH

150 Stretch your left hand under your right wrist. Open your right fist and turn the palms up, separate your hands until they are shoulder-width apart and pull them back.

151 Sit back onto your right foot, with the toes of your left foot raised. Pull your hands down to your waist.

152 Complete the left bow step and push your palms forward and up to shoulder height, palms facing out. Look between your hands (to 9 o'clock).

POINTS TO REMEMBER

Do not lean backward when sitting back. Keep your seat tucked in. Relax your shoulders and turn your elbows slightly out as you pull back your arms as your body moves. Do not pull your arms back straight. Your hands should be shoulder-width apart.

The 24 steps of the form flow into one another to become one seamless movement, performed at a constant speed.

㉓ CROSS HANDS

153 Shift your weight onto your right foot. Turn to the right and pivot on your left toes.

154 Circle your hands to shoulder height, palms forward, elbows slightly bent. Turn your right toes out, and shift your weight onto your right foot. Look at your right hand.

157 You are facing 12 o'clock. Separate your hands, keeping them at shoulder height. Look forward. You are now in the starting position of the form.

POINTS TO REMEMBER

Do not lean forward when separating or crossing your hands. When making the parallel stance, keep your body naturally straight, with your head suspended and your chin tucked slightly inward. Keep your arms rounded in a comfortable position, with your shoulders and elbows down.

155 Shift your weight to your left foot, and turn your right toes in. Bring the right foot toward your left foot, so that you are standing in shoulder-width stance.

156 Straighten your legs and lower both hands and cross them in front of you. Raise them to your chest, with your wrists at shoulder height, your right hand on the outside, both palms facing in.

24 CLOSING FORM

158 Turn your palms forward and down while lowering both arms gradually to the side of your hips.

159 Keep your entire body relaxed and draw a deep, prolonged breath as you lower your hands. Continue to look straight ahead to 12 o'clock. You may now commence another round of the form.

Twenty-Four Step Tai Chi Chuan – The Complete

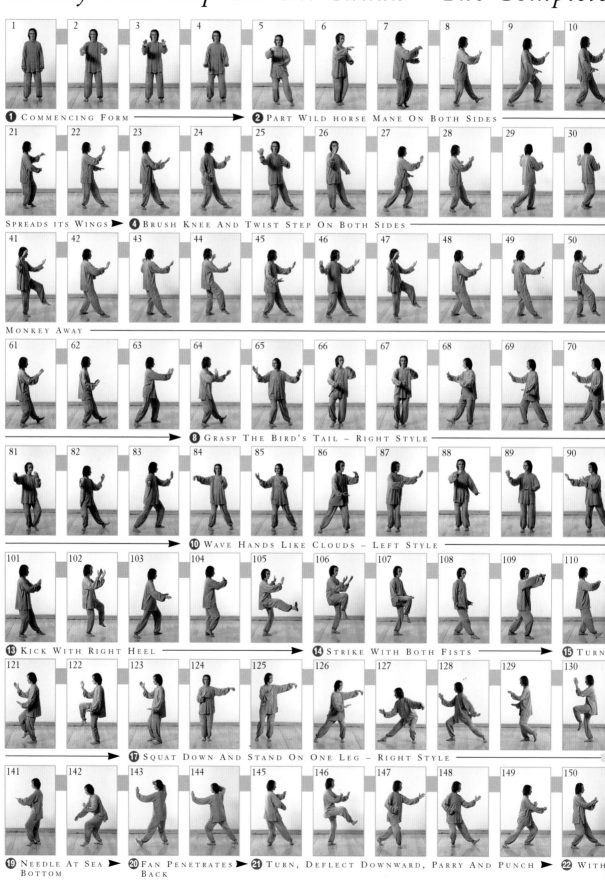

1 COMMENCING FORM ⟶ **2** PART WILD HORSE MANE ON BOTH SIDES

SPREADS ITS WINGS ▶ **4** BRUSH KNEE AND TWIST STEP ON BOTH SIDES

MONKEY AWAY

8 GRASP THE BIRD'S TAIL – RIGHT STYLE

10 WAVE HANDS LIKE CLOUDS – LEFT STYLE

13 KICK WITH RIGHT HEEL ⟶ **14** STRIKE WITH BOTH FISTS ▶ **15** TURN

17 SQUAT DOWN AND STAND ON ONE LEG – RIGHT STYLE

19 NEEDLE AT SEA BOTTOM   **20** FAN PENETRATES BACK ▶ **21** TURN, DEFLECT DOWNWARD, PARRY AND PUNCH ▶ **22** WITH

Sequence

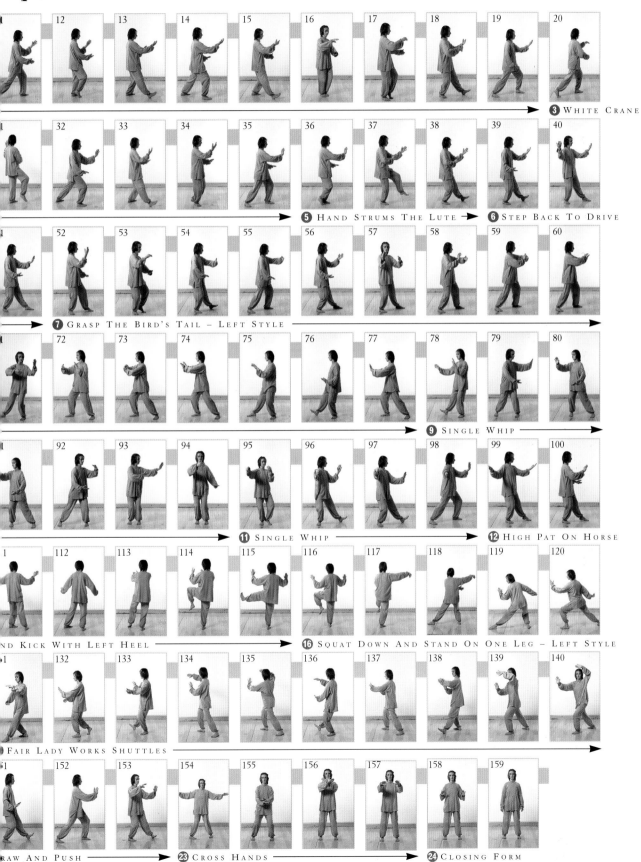

3 WHITE CRANE

5 HAND STRUMS THE LUTE → 6 STEP BACK TO DRIVE

7 GRASP THE BIRD'S TAIL – LEFT STYLE

9 SINGLE WHIP

11 SINGLE WHIP → 12 HIGH PAT ON HORSE

ND KICK WITH LEFT HEEL → 16 SQUAT DOWN AND STAND ON ONE LEG – LEFT STYLE

FAIR LADY WORKS SHUTTLES

RAW AND PUSH → 23 CROSS HANDS → 24 CLOSING FORM

Two-person Practice
- Strength through Softness

THE TAI CHI form has its roots in the Chinese martial arts tradition, in which testing yourself against an opponent is the best way of discovering how far you have progressed. But unlike the "hard" styles of kung-fu, in which the aim is to knock down an opponent with the sheer brute strength of a punch or kick, tai chi uses softness as its main weapon; it yields to pressure and deflects blows, and turns their power against the aggressor. This principle is epitomized by a saying of the great tai chi teacher, Wang Zongyue (1736–1795), "From the sentence 'a force of four ounces deflects a thousand pounds' we know that the technique is not accomplished through strength."

Two-person practice (also known as push-hands) is not intended to show how strong you have become, but to reveal the exact opposite: to see if you are able to yield completely to your partner's movements, never presenting a square inch of hardness on your body. In this way, you learn to "read" your partner's movements.

In the early stages of tai chi study, two-person practice is an invaluable help in discovering any faults in your performance of the form. Are your feet properly rooted to the ground? Does you waist turn freely? Are your shoulders and arms rounded and relaxed? If your feet are unbalanced, then your partner can easily push you over; and if your waist or arms are stiff, he or she can use them as levers to topple you.

SINGLE CIRCLING HANDS

1 Stand facing your partner with your feet shoulder-width apart and your right foot forward and your left foot turned out. Bend your knees. Your partner mirrors your stance with his right foot forward. Your bodies should be approximately three feet (one meter) apart.

2 Raise your right arm in front of your chest, keeping your shoulder and elbow relaxed and rounded. Make contact with your partner's raised arm lightly with the back of your hand, near his or her wrist. Shift your weight from your left to your right foot, rocking your body backward and forward.

3 Keep both feet flat on the floor and, at this stage, do not let your body rise or fall during the movement. When you move forward, do not push against your partner's hand, merely follow him as he retreats.

*"**A** nyone who has spent years and still cannot neutralize has not apprehended the fault of double-weightedness."*

- WANG ZONGYUE

4 Once you and your partner are comfortable with the forward and backward motion, turn your waist and make a circular motion with your hand.

5 Your partner follows with the same movement. Remember to keep your knees bent, and focus your mind in your body's center of gravity, your *dantian*. In tai chi chuan push-hands, the aim is to find a place of hardness in your partner's body and use it to topple him. But for your practice, concentrate on your own movements and faults.

6 After 10–15 minutes, repeat with your left foot forward, circling with your right arm.

DOUBLE CIRCLING HANDS

*"I*n push-hands the hands are not needed. The whole body is a hand and the hand is not a hand.*"*

- CHENG MANQING

1 Once you and your partner are moving freely in the one-handed practice, you can attempt the two-handed version shown here. In the same stance as in the one-handed form, link both hands lightly near the wrists.

2 Shift your weight from your front to rear foot. Add the rotation of your waist as before.

3 Make a circular motion with your hands, extending your arms as you lean forward and withdrawing them as you lean back.

3 You may, at this stage, wish to challenge your partner to try to "uproot" you. This does not mean he or she has to pick you up and throw you to the floor, but to try and find a place of hardness in your body to get you off balance. As you practice, keep your mind centered in your *dantian*.

4 When it is your turn to extend, imagine your qi traveling up along your spine, to your shoulders, along your arms and out of your hands. Practice both the one- and two-handed two-person exercises with your eyes closed to enable you to use your sense of touch only to gauge your partner's movements.

"Attract to emptiness and discharge; attach without losing attachment."

– SONG OF HAND PUSHING

5 If you try to push your partner with brute force, he or she will make use of the hardness you manifest to push or pull you off balance. After 10–15 minutes, repeat with the opposite leg forward.

*U*ntamed, the mind is your greatest enemy:
crippled by self-doubt, beset by irrational fears,
and divided by its own conflicting desires.
In meditation you will find
the inner peace that alone
can give you clarity,
simplicity and
happiness.

Meditation

Introducing meditation

WE ALL HAVE moments when we are so busy that we have to sit down and gather our thoughts for a few seconds. It is this same natural impulse that prompted our ancestors to begin meditating. Meditation is usually thought of as a spiritual exercise leading to enlightenment, but tai chi has discovered its practical dimension, which you can use, regardless of your religious beliefs, to improve your mental well-being. As a means of taking control of your thoughts and feelings, meditation is an ideal exercise to overcome the stress of modern-day life.

Buddhist zazen and *Christian prayer lead to spiritual insight, but meditation also has a role to play in helping us find our mental equilibrium.*

Stress is a mental condition that produces physical symptoms. Among the most common are sleeplessness, eating disorders and tiredness. We can deal with the symptoms of stress with medicines, but this is often at the cost of adding side-effects, or if the symptoms are serious, drug dependence to our original problems. The only real cure for stress is to tackle its root causes, which are mental.

ONE-POINTED MIND

In daily life, our attention always seems divided, confused, harassed. Yet we are not taught techniques that will help us detach ourselves from the worries and pressures of our home and professional lives. In its simplest form, meditation is making time for a moment of peace in our busy routine. To meditate, all you need to do is go to a tranquil place, close your eyes and clear your mind of all thoughts – good or bad. But to get the full benefits of meditation, you must not regard it as a passive activity like taking a catnap. Its ultimate aim is to give you the calmness and focus of the one-pointed mind that will enable you to control your thoughts and allow you to attain your full potential. In the beginning, you must be prepared to train your undisciplined mind as hard as you would train your unfit body.

The opportunity to meditate are all around you: inspire yourself with the contemplation of the beauty and tranquillity of nature.

STILLNESS IN MOTION

If you have attempted some of the exercises described in the earlier chapters of this book, you will know that tai chi is a unique combination of physical exercise and mental concentration, mediated and unified through the ancient Chinese concept of qi. As such, it is the ideal antidote both to the physical symptoms of stress, as well as a way to deal with its mental causes. Stress becomes locked in our bodies in the form of tension in our muscles and joints, and unless it is released, it will damage us and lead to physical injury and illness.

All forms of movement, including dance, fitness training and sport, help us to deal with the physical symptoms of stress, because they allow us to release some of the tension locked in our bodies; however, as maintaining or restoring the holistic health of mind and body is not their primary function, their effectiveness remains limited. In fact, certain forms of conventional exercise, such as competitive sport and professional ballet, which are mentally and physically very stressful, may make the problem worse.

Tai chi employs a range of meditation techniques, some of which you will recognize from other traditions, such as hatha and tantric yoga, but it is in its joyous use of movement that it excels them all.

Mental stress becomes locked in our bodies and the easiest way to release it and prevent it from regaining its grip is through physical movement.

Moving Meditation

Link your hands, breathe in and stretch your arms over your head, releasing the tension in your upper back and shoulders.

LIFE IS MOVEMENT, and the only true stillness is in death. Even when we are asleep, the continuous processes of life cause the tissues of our bodies to be renewed and repaired, and our minds to be refreshed through dreams.

People often confuse meditation with trance, in which you give up control of your body, and sometimes of your conscious self, to another person or an external force, such as a mind-altering drug. The aim of meditation is the exact opposite: to give you complete control over your mind, and through your mind of your body.

All forms of meditation need a focus to still the mind, and later in this chapter, we will see how this can be achieved with breathing and visualization techniques. But we will begin with tai chi's unique contribution to the world: moving meditation.

"We look at it and do not see it; Its name is the Invisible. We listen to it but do not hear it. Its name is the inaudible."

— TAO TEH CHING

"*To hold and fill a cup to overflowing is not as good as stopping in time.*"

– TAO TEH CHING

THE JOYOUS DANCE

Our bodies are not only designed to move, but also to enjoy movement. It is no accident that many of our most pleasurable and joyful activities – dancing, sport and making love – fully engage our minds, senses and bodies in harmonious movement. The tai chi chuan form itself is often described as a moving meditation, but its function is to combine body and mind to circulate and increase the qi, in order to maintain and improve physical health. In moving meditation, the emphasis is reversed, and the motions of the body becomes the agent to center the mind.

As such, you are freed from the constraints of following the exact and demanding movements and sequence of the form. You can let your body experience the complete joyfulnesss of unfettered movement. Where the form provides a discipline, moving meditation offers a joyous release of limitations – an invitation to explore and expand the boundaries of your physical being.

Let your body move from position to position smoothly. Breathe in as you stretch up and out and in as you pull down and in. Keep your mind focused in your *dantian*, your body's center of gravity.

"*Thirty spokes are united to make a wheel but it is on its non-being that the utility of the carriage depends, therefore turn being into advantage and non-being into utility.*"

- TAO TEH CHING

When performing the automatic motion exercise, the movements you will experience range from gentle swaying to dynamic jumps and arm swings.

AUTOMATIC MOTION

You may have heard of automatic writing, in which you temporarily relinquish voluntary command of your actions; in automatic motion, you let your qi take over your body's movements. It is a particularly helpful exercise to those who have difficulty letting go of their bodies.

Stand relaxed in shoulder-width stance, with your arms relaxed. Take a few deep breaths to clear your mind, and center your attention in your *dantian*. Tap your navel with the fingers of your right hand and rub the top of your head with your left index finger three times to start the flow of qi.

Perform six to nine repetitions of three of the tai chi qigong exercises, just as you would in your daily practice. When you have finished stand easy and imagine the qi flowing down from your head and up from the soles of your feet. Allow your body to move at will, but remember that your movements can become expansive and dynamic. If you become worried, focus your mind to bring your body gently to a halt.

Preparations for Moving Meditation

Y OU DO NOT need to study to attempt moving meditation; there are no complicated movements or sequences, no secret words or formulas to memorize. You stand like the first human, with only your mind, your body and the Universe around you.

As long as you are not exposed to extremes of heat or cold, you may prefer to perform this exercise clothed or naked, indoors or outdoors. All you require is a quiet space in which you feel completely comfortable, and that is large enough so that you take ten or so steps in any direction and swing your arms without coming into contact with any obstacles.

STILLING THE HEART

Begin the meditation standing or kneeling in the center of your chosen space, and close your eyes. Center your mind in your *dantian*. Your first task is to regulate your breathing. Breathe slowly and evenly, taking air in through your nose and expelling it through your mouth. Try and make the in and out breath last the same time, but without straining. As you breathing settles, notice how the beating of your heart slows to match it. Breathe for at least ten full breaths before moving on to the next stage.

UNLOCK THE GATES

The next stage is to relax every muscle in your body and open every joint, so that the qi can

"*M*anifest plainness, embrace simplicity."

-TAO TEH CHING

Begin your moving meditation practice by regulating your breathing and then consciously relaxing your whole body.

SOME GENTLE CAUTIONS

In moving meditation, you may find your body moving in dynamic patterns. Should your movements become too rapid and expansive, immediately focus with your mind to regain control and slow yourself down. Remember that you are always in charge. Settle yourself and then resume the exercise.

If you feel self-conscious about moving meditation, begin moving to a favorite piece of music, but do not focus on the music but on the movements themselves.

flow freely. Start with the muscles of your face and neck. Pay particular attention to the shoulders and upper back, where tension accumulates. Relax your arms, from the shoulders to the hands and down to the tiny muscles of the fingers. As you feel the tension leave you, imagine the qi flowing freely through the joints of your upper spine, shoulders and arms. Let all the tension out of your upper body, and then from your legs, opening the joints of you lower spine, hips and knees, until you reach your feet and toes. Your whole body should now feel relaxed, but do not let your posture slump. Keep your head suspended and your back erect.

DANCE DANCE DANCE

When your body is relaxed, return your mind to your *dantian*. From this point on, you are free to choose your movements. You may wish to inspire yourself from the tai chi form or the qigong exercises, or from other forms of exercise and dance that you have taken part in; or you may want to listen to your body, and let your qi alone guide you. This free-form meditation is particularly beneficial for those in sedentary jobs, who cannot release physical stress in their work.

Sitting and Standing

STILL MEDITATION IS without doubt the most difficult exercise to perform. In moving meditation, your mind is centered by the gentle rhythms of your qi, but when your body is forced to be immobile and your senses are shut off, your mind becomes bored and craves any distraction. Still meditation uses techniques to focus the mind to attain a state of inner peace. A common technique is to concentrate on your own breathing, which slows the heart and relaxes the body, while the improved flow of oxygen sharpens the mind; another is creative visualization, in which the mind creates an imaginary place or sensation as the anchoring point of the mind.

One of the traditional poses for yoga meditation and breathing exercises is the lotus position. In this variant, the half lotus, only one leg is held in place.

"Exhibit the unadorned and embrace the uncarved block. Have little thought of self and as few desires as possible."

— TAO TEH CHING

*"*H*e who conquers others has physical strength. He who conquers himself is strong."*

- TAO TEH CHING

SITTING MEDITATION

If you have difficulty in sitting on the floor, you can practice meditation sitting in a chair. Do not attempt this exercise on a sofa or armchair because your will not be able to maintain the correct position of your back and head, and are more likely to fall asleep.

1 Sit with your back straight in a chair, with your feet flat on the floor. Place your hands on your thighs, and close your eyes. When you breathe in pull in your stomach by contracting your abdominal muscles. Hold for a count of two and breathe out, relaxing your stomach muscles.

2 Do not let your chin drop forward or your shoulders slump, as this will impede your breathing, and gradually break your concentration. Keep the mind focused on the inhalation and contraction, and the exhalation and relaxation. Continue for 10–12 full breath cycles.

Yin/Yang Breathing Exercise

Breathing is overlooked by conventional exercise methods, which limit themselves to encouraging us to "take a deep breath," when our lungs feel as if they're about to burst. But as the means our bodies obtain life-giving oxygen and expel toxins, it has long been recognized in India and China as a vital ingredient of fitness. The Indian yogic breathing techniques known as pranayama *were imported to China with the Buddhist religion, and in the intervening centuries, the Chinese refined them into their own system of breathing exercises to increase health and vitality. The following two exercises will improve your breathing function and will enable you to center your mind during meditation.*

1 Stand with your feet slightly apart and your arms hanging by your sides. Hold your head and upper back straight. Close your eyes if it aids your concentration. Breathe through your nose for a count of five to eight seconds. Imagine that the air is like water being poured into a jar. Your abdomen fills first and then your chest. Hold your breath for a count of two seconds before breathing out through your mouth for a count of five to eight. Imagine that you are emptying the jar of water from the top of the chest to the bottom of your abdomen. Continue for 10–12 full breath cycles.

2 Close your eyes and breathe out, but imagine that you are holding back half of the out-breath in your stomach. Breathe in and out again, expelling the old half of the air you held back on the previous out-breath, and taking in a new half breath of air. Continue this pattern for 10–12 full cycles.

"*The qi should be excited, the spirit should be internally gathered.*"

- Zhang Sanfeng

STANDING – THE WATERFALL METHOD

Another technique used to center the mind during meditation is creative visualization. In this exercise the soothing power of water is used as the focus to aid concentration.

1 In a quiet place, stand in a relaxed stance and close your eyes. Imagine that you are standing in a shallow pool of warm water. You step under a gentle waterfall.

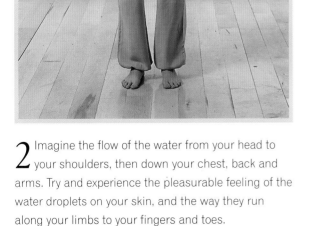

"*Be as still as a mountain, move like a great river.*"

- WU YUXIANG

2 Imagine the flow of the water from your head to your shoulders, then down your chest, back and arms. Try and experience the pleasurable feeling of the water droplets on your skin, and the way they run along your limbs to your fingers and toes.

CAUTION

While breathing and visualization exercises do not seem to be strenuous, they may have unexpected physical effects, such as light-headedness and giddiness. If this happens, discontinue the exercise and sit quietly for a moment before resuming.

STANDING STILL TO KEEP FIT

Practice of the form makes demands on your legs because it is performed with bent knees, which quickly tires the muscles of your hips and thighs. If the weakness of your legs is limiting the time you can spend practicing, one of the easiest ways to strengthen them is by performing the standing exercises below. If you wish to practice discreetly in a line or other public place, stand easy, hands by your side, shift your weight to one foot and bend your knees. As soon as one leg is tired, shift weight to the other foot.

"*He who stands on tiptoe is not steady.*"

- TAO TEH CHING

1 Stand with your feet shoulder-width apart and bend the knees. Raise both arms in front of you, keeping the elbows soft and rounded, as if you were hugging a tree. Keep your shoulders relaxed, not allowing any tension to build up in your neck and back. Feel your feet sink into the ground and become rooted, as if you were becoming part of the tree. Hold for 5–10 minutes.

2 Stand in the Hand Strums the Lute posture of the simplified form (page 65). Close your eyes and hold the pose for 5–10 minutes, then shake out any tension and repeat with the opposite arm and leg.

3 Helping yourself with your hands, lift your right leg and place your right foot against your left thigh. Press your palms together in front of your chest. Hold the position for 5 minutes and repeat with your left leg.

"*A journey of a thousand leagues begins with but a single step.*"

- TAO TEH CHING

Index

Credits

Quarto Publishing would like to thank the following for providing photographs and for permission to reproduce copyright material. While every effort has been made to trace and acknowledge all copyright holders, we would like to apologize should any omissions have been made.

Key
l = left   r = right
b = bottom   t = top

e. t. archive: 11b; Image Bank: 6r, 8b, 112tr, 113b; Image Select: 10b; Pictor: 6l, 7, 9r, 10t, 116, 120b, 125; Tony Stone Worldwide: 8t, 12b, 117b, 119b, 121t, 122; Visual Arts Library: 9b

All other pictures are the copyright of Quarto Publishing plc.

Quotes on pages 10, 11, 12, 17, 26, 27, 35, 41, 45, 48, 107, 108, 109, 122, 123 from *The Essence of Tai Chi Ch'uan: The Literary Tradition*, translated and edited by Benjamin Lo, Martin Inn, Robert Amacker, Susan Foe. Copyright © 1979 by Benjamin Lo, Martin Inn, Robert Amacker, Susan Foe. Used by permission of North Atlantic Books, Berkeley, California, USA.

Index provided by Dawn Butcher